Understanding Differences

Some Kids Use
Wheelchairs

Revised Edition

Lola M Schaefer

raintree

a Capstone company — publishers for children

Raintree is an imprint of Capstone Global Library Limited,
a company incorporated in England and Wales having its
registered office at 264 Banbury Road, Oxford, OX2 7DY –
Registered company number: 6695582

www.raintree.co.uk
myorders@raintree.co.uk

Editorial credits
Sarah Bennett, designer; Tracy Cummins, media researcher;
Laura Manthe, production specialist

Photo credits
Capstone Studio: Karon Dubke, 7, 13, 15, 17, 19; Getty Images:
KidStock, 9; Newscom: Leah Warkentin/Design Pics, 21;
Shutterstock: Jaren Jai Wicklund, Cover, 5, 11

Printed and bound in India

ISBN 978 1 4747 5689 1
22 21 20 19 18
10 9 8 7 6 5 4 3 2 1

British Library Cataloguing in Publication Data
A full catalogue record for this book is available from the
British Library.

Contents

Why kids use wheelchairs

Some kids use wheelchairs.

Kids who cannot walk use

wheelchairs to get around.

Some kids cannot walk because

they were born with weak

bones or muscles.

Other kids use wheelchairs

after they have been injured.

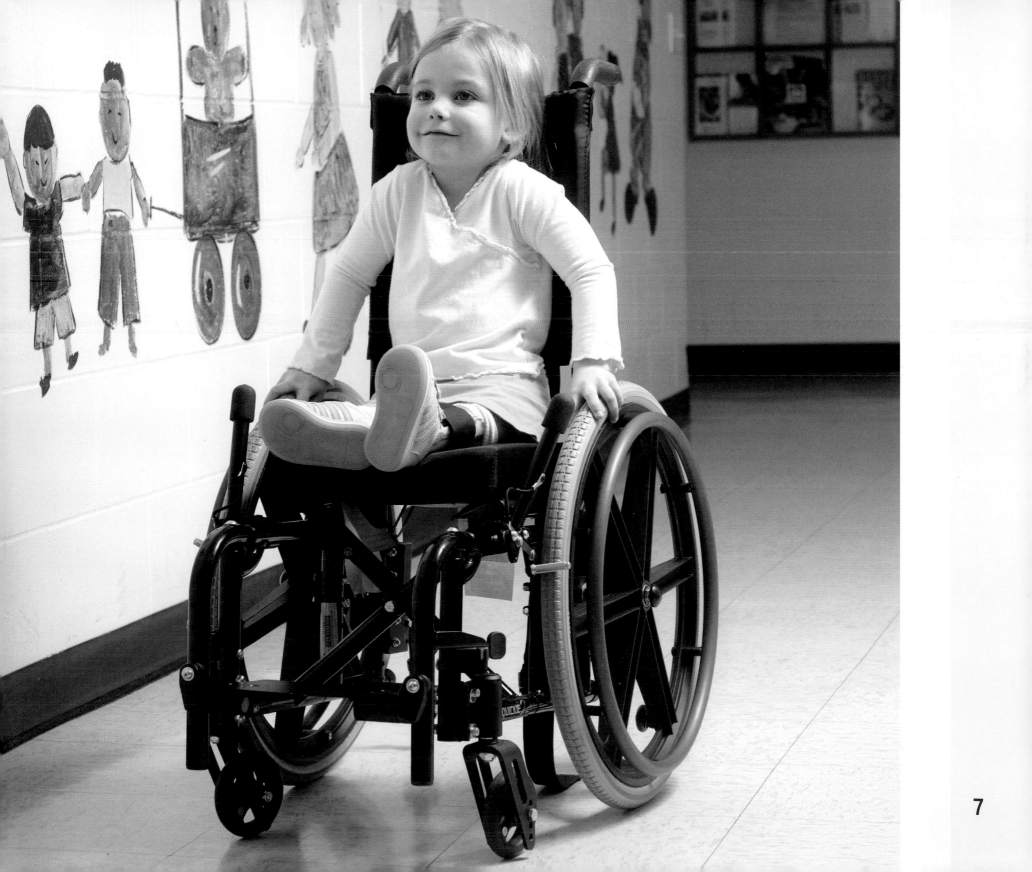

Being active

Physiotherapists help kids who use wheelchairs to stretch their muscles.

Some kids who use wheelchairs go swimming. The exercise is good for their muscles.

Everyday life

Kids who use wheelchairs

go to many places.

They use ramps to get

into vans.

They use ramps to enter and exit buildings.

Kids who use wheelchairs

go to the library.

They read books and

use computers.

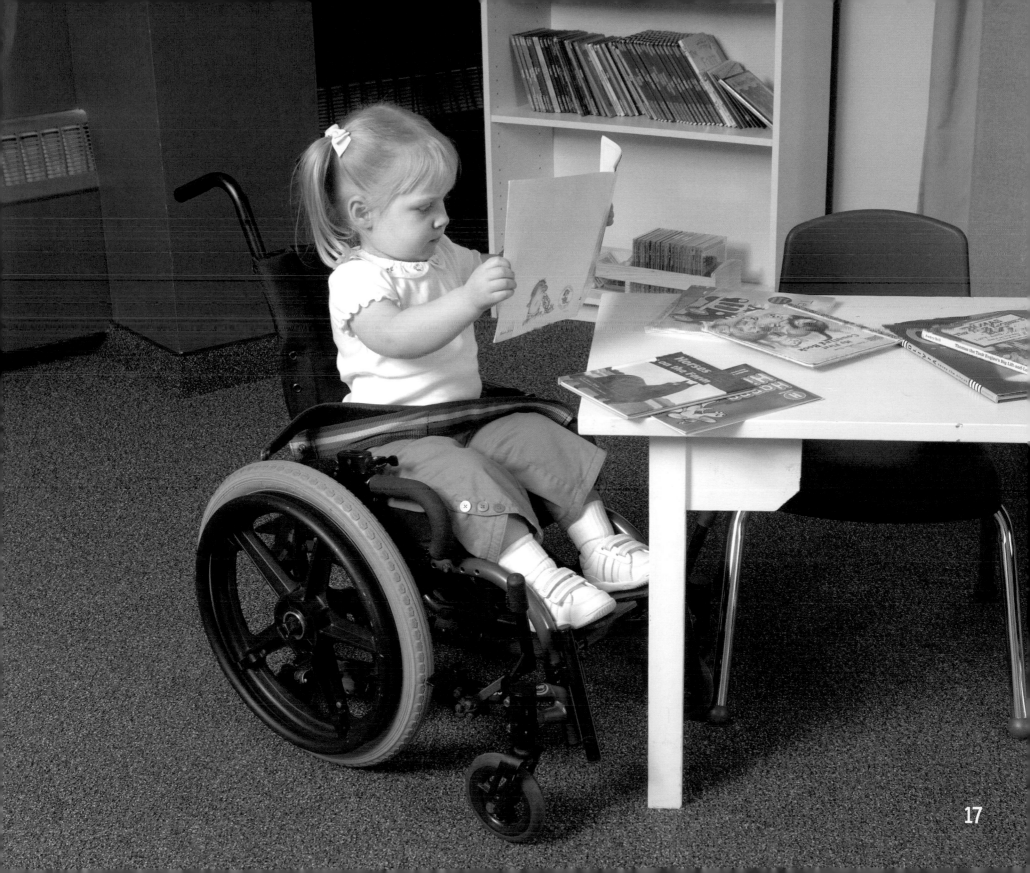

Some kids who use wheelchairs

play sports.

Some kids who use wheelchairs

go skateboarding.

They have fun!

Glossary

physiotherapist person trained to give treatment to people who are hurt or have physical disabilities; massage and exercise are two kinds of treatment

ramp flat area that slants to connect two levels; ramps allow people in wheelchairs to get into buildings and vans

wheelchair type of chair on wheels for people who are ill, injured or have physical disabilities; wheelchairs can be pushed by hand or by motor

Find out more

Books

Having a Disability (Questions and Feelings About), Louise Spilsbury (Franklin Watts, 2017)

We All Have Different Abilities (Celebrating Differences), Melissa Higgins (Raintree, 2017)

Websites

Find out what it's like to live with a disabled brother: https://www.bbc.co.uk/education/clips/ztbfb9q

Information about living with a disabled sibling: https://www.sibs.org.uk/

A charity that helps improve the lives of children who use wheelchairs: http://www.whizz-kidz.org.uk/about-us

Comprehension questions

1. What does a physiotherapist do?

2. What are some reasons a person may need to use a wheelchair?

3. Why are ramps important to people who use wheelchairs?

Index